Addition

Written By:
Kim Mitzo Thompson
Karen Mitzo Hilderbrand

Illustrated By:
Betsy Snyder

Cover Illustration By:
Sandy Haight

Twin 443 – Addition (Tape/Book Set) –   ISBN# 1-57583-314-X
                    (CD/Book Set) –   ISBN# 1-57583-332-8

Copyright © 2001 Kim Mitzo Thompson and Karen Mitzo Hilderbrand, Twin Sisters Productions, Inc. All rights reserved. No part of this publication may be reproduced, stored in a retrieval system, or transmitted in any form electronic, mechanical, photocopying, recording, or otherwise, without written permission of the copyright owners. Permission is hereby granted, with the purchase of one copy of **Addition**, to reproduce the worksheets for use in the classroom.

Twin Sisters Productions, Inc. • (800) 248-TWIN • www.twinsisters.com

Table of Contents

Addition Lyrics
Take Me Out To The Ball Game..3
It's A Home Run..4
The Island Of Learning..5
The Two-More-Than Strategy...6
I'm Jumpin' To The Beat Of The Music...7
What Do You Say?..8
The Fabulous Family Of Fives..9
I'm Hooked..10
Over And Over And Over Again..11
While We Exercise...12
It's Time To Review...13
I'm Talkin' About Doubles..14
Doubles Plus One..15

Addition Practice Pages
Number Line Addition (Sums to 10)...16
Find The Secret Message (Sums to 12)..17
Greater Than/Less Than..18
Adding Doubles...19
Doubles Plus One Practice..20
At The Baseball Game...21

Time Tests
Sums to 12...22
Sums to 18...23
Answer Key..24

 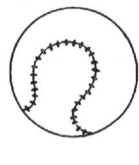 

Take Me Out To The Ball Game

What an exciting game! All afternoon we've been battling to stay alive, and now, at the bottom of the 9th, we have a chance. The score is tied 6 to 6 and there are 2 outs. What's it gonna be? The pitch! It's going, it's going... it's out of here! It's a home run! We've won the game!

Take me out to the ball game.
Take me out to the park.
Buy me some peanuts and cracker jacks.
I don't care if I ever get back.

Oh, we'll root, root, root, for the home team.
If they don't win it's a shame.
For it's one, two, three strikes—you're out
at the old ball game.

It's A Home Run

**Be a home run hitter, be part of the team,
be a quick base runner, and you will succeed.
For if you practice hard in sports and school,
you will be a winner. Let determination rule!**

Practice how to throw the ball,
practice how to catch,
and let your coaches teach you all the rest.
Math facts, fast balls, grounders, winning scores,
it's really all the same. Let's hear some more!

When you're adding zeros,
there's nothing you can do
but stay on that number.
Here's a little clue:
any number added to zero stays the same.
Let's practice this rule. It's an addition game.

0+1 is 1   0+6 is 6
0+2 is 2   0+7 is 7
0+3 is 3   0+8 is 8
0+4 is 4   0+9 is 9
0+5 is 5

(Chorus)

Now we're moving up.
Let's add the facts of one.
Another trick to learn.
We're having so much fun.
Take any number and then add one more.
You'll realize you count up one and no more.

1+1 is 2   1+6 is 7
1+2 is 3   1+7 is 8
1+3 is 4   1+8 is 9
1+4 is 5   1+9 is 10
1+5 is 6

(Chorus)

Once you know the rules
of a baseball game,
and strategies to help you
in adding–
I'll proclaim–practice makes
you better.
Yes, it's the only way.
So we'll mix up the facts,
and really concentrate.

1+8 is 9
0+5 is 5
1+3 is 4
0+7 is 7
0+2 is 2
1+9 is 10
1+1 is 2
0+8 is 8
1+2 is 3

(Chorus)

©Twin Sisters Productions, Inc.　　　　TWIN 443 - Addition

The Island Of Learning

**Clap your hands and move with me
as we travel to the island of learning,
where adventure and knowledge you'll find.
It's a place that'll captivate your mind.**

(Repeat)

It's time to do the limbo dance.
It's time to swing and move.
It's time to learn our facts of two
as we sing to the rhythmic groove.

2+1 is 3 and 2+2 is 4
Let us move the limbo stick
closer to the floor.

2+3 is 5 and 2+4 is 6
Gather as we do the dance
with our limbo stick.

(Chorus)

2+5 is 7 and 2+6 is 8
Bend your back and head real low.
Do not hesitate.

2+7 is 9 and 2+8 is 10
Now you've got the limbo down.
Let's do it all again.

2+9 is 11
Let's take it from the top and say our
facts as we do the dance
'til it's time to stop.

(Chorus)

2+1 is 3
2+2 is 4
2+3 is 5
2+4 is 6
2+5 is 7
2+6 is 8
2+7 is 9
2+8 is 10
2+9 is 11

(Chorus 2x)

©Twin Sisters Productions, Inc.

TWIN 443 - Addition

The Two-More-Than Strategy

I'm going to teach you a simple strategy. When you're adding any number plus 2, just think "two-more-than" that number, or that number plus 2, and you will solve the problem easily. This is called the **two-more-than** strategy. Let's play a little game while we learn more about this strategy.

**It's the two-more-than, the two-more-than, the two-more-than strategy.
It will help you add when one number is a two.
It's a wonderful plan. You'll see.**

Let's take a number—how about 3?—
and apply my simple rule.
Think "two-more-than" and what do you get? 5.
It's an awesome learning tool.

I say a number, and I want you to think
the two-more-than strategy.
Just move up two and you'll be right.
It makes learning fun indeed!

I say 6	think two more	6+2 is 8
I say 2	think two more	2+2 is 4
I say 7	think two more	7+2 is 9
I say 4	think two more	4+2 is 6

(Chorus)

I say 3	think two more	3+2 is 5
I say 8	think two more	8+2 is 10
I say 5	think two more	5+2 is 7
I say 9	think two more	9+2 is 11

If you see a problem and one number is a two,
just apply my simple rule.
Think "two-more-than" and the answer you'll know.
It's a wonderful learning tool.

(Chorus)

**It will help you add when one number is a two.
It's a wonderful plan. You'll see.**

I'm Jumpin' To The Beat Of The Music

**I'm jumpin' to the beat of the music.
I'm jumpin' to the beat of the song.
Yeah, I'm jumpin' to the beat of the music.
Won't you come with me and jump along?**

(Repeat)

Yeah, I'm jumpin' up high, I'm clappin' down low.
I'm turning around and I'm touchin' my toes.
I'm reaching real high and I'm givin' a wave
as I'm learnin' all my facts today.

3+1 is 4

3+2 is 5

3+3 is 6

3+4 is 7

(Chorus)

3+5 is 8

3+6 is 9

3+7 is 10

3+8 is 11

(Chorus)

3+9 is 12

(Chorus)

Yeah, I'm jumpin' up high, I'm clappin' down low.
I'm turning around and I'm touchin' my toes.
I'm reaching real high and I'm givin' a wave
as I'm learnin' all my facts today.

Jumpin' to the beat of the music.

What Do You Say?

What do you say?
What do you say?

What do you say?
What do you say?
Let's learn our facts.
You'll be amazed.
What do you say?
What do you say?
Come, let's practice your facts today.

4+1 is 5   4+6 is 10
4+2 is 6   4+7 is 11
4+3 is 7   4+8 is 12
4+4 is 8   4+9 is 13
4+5 is 9

What do you say?
What do you say?
Let's learn our facts.
Now do you dare?
What do you say?
What do you say?
Come, let's practice—and be prepared.

4+1 is 5   4+6 is 10
4+2 is 6   4+7 is 11
4+3 is 7   4+8 is 12
4+4 is 8   4+9 is 13
4+5 is 9

What do you say?
What do you say?
Let's mix up the facts
before we start.
What do you say?
What do you say?
Shout the answers.
I know you're smart.

4+3 is...
4+9 is...
4+6 is...
4+7 is...

What do you say?
What do you say?
Are you ready for more?
Can you add today?
What do you say?
What do you say?
Shout the answers,
now don't delay.

4+9 is...
4+2 is...
4+5 is...
4+8 is...

What do you say?
What do you say?
You learned the 4s—
an accomplishment!
What do you say?
What do you say?
You are truly magnificent!

What do you say?

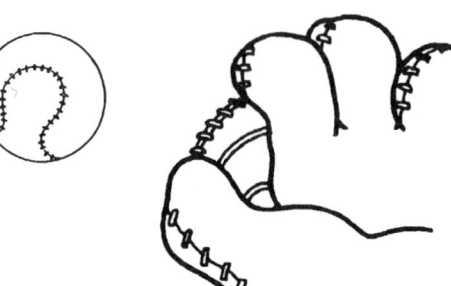

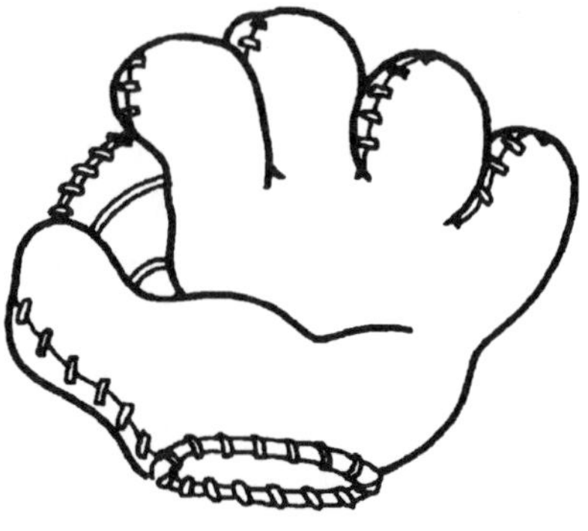

©Twin Sisters Productions, Inc.

TWIN 443 - Addition

The Fabulous Family Of Fives

When you are learning addition facts, the numbers to be added together are called **addends**. The answer is called the **sum**. You can change the order of the addends around, but the sum will remain the same.

You can change the addends all around;
the sum remains the same.
You can add two numbers any which way;
the answer still remains the same.

Let's say the facts of five and then
we'll change the numbers around.
We'll learn our fabulous fives.
They're the coolest thing in town.

**It's the fab, fab, fab, fab,
fabulous family of fives.
Fabulous family of fives.
It's the fab, fab, fab, fab,
fabulous family of fives.
Fabulous family of fives.
We are featuring the friendly,
famously fine,
fan, fantastic, enthusiastic,
fab, fab, fab, fab,
fabulous family of fives.
Fabulous family of fives.**

5+1 is 6
5+2 is 7
5+3 is 8
5+4 is 9
5+5 is 10

Let's say the facts of five and then
we'll change the numbers around.
We'll learn our fabulous fives.
They're the coolest thing in town.

1+5 is 6
2+5 is 7
3+5 is 8
4+5 is 9
5+5 is 10

(Chorus)

You can change
the addends all around;
the sum remains the same.
You can add two numbers
any which way;
the answer still remains the same.

Let's move up to the higher facts,
then we'll change
the numbers around.
We'll learn our fabulous fives.
They're the coolest thing in town.

(Chorus)

5+6 is 11
5+7 is 12
5+8 is 13
5+9 is 14

Let's say the facts of five
and then we'll change
the numbers around.
We'll learn our fabulous fives.
They're the coolest thing in town.

6+5 is 11
7+5 is 12
8+5 is 13
9+5 is 14

(Chorus)

©Twin Sisters Productions, Inc.   TWIN 443 - Addition

I'm Hooked

I am hooked on learnin'.
I am hooked on math.
I am hooked on learnin' my addition facts.
I'm feelin' kind of brainy 'cause I'm doing my part
to learn my 6s.
Now I'm hooked on being smart!

6+1 is 7
6+2 is 8
6+3 is 9
6+4 is 10
6+5 is 11
6+6 is 12
6+7 is 13
6+8 is 14
6+9 is 15

Now I'm hooked on being smart!
Now I'm hooked on being smart!
Now I'm hooked on being smart!

I'm hooked!

I am hooked on learnin'.
I'll tell it to you straight.
If you study real hard and you concentrate.
Are you feelin' kind of brainy?
Are you ready to start?
Let's learn the 6s.
Now get hooked on being smart!

6+1 is 7
6+2 is 8
6+3 is 9
6+4 is 10
6+5 is 11
6+6 is 12
6+7 is 13
6+8 is 14
6+9 is 15

(Chorus)

©Twin Sisters Productions, Inc.

TWIN 443 - Addition

Over And Over And Over Again

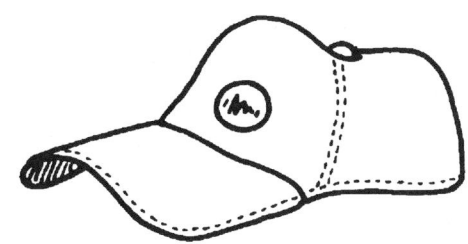

Over and over and over again.
Over and over and over and then
we'll learn our facts—if we repeat each
one over and over again.
(Repeat)

7+1 is 8
7+2 is 9
7+3 is 10
Let's say them over and over again.

7+1 is 8
7+2 is 9
7+3 is 10
You won't hear the answers,
but say them again.

7+1 is...
7+2 is...
7+3 is...

(Chorus)

7+4 is 11
7+5 is 12
7+6 is 13
Let's say them over and over again.

7+4 is 11
7+5 is 12
7+6 is 13
You won't hear the answers,
but say them again.

7+4 is...
7+5 is...
7+6 is...

(Chorus)

7+7 is 14
7+8 is 15
7+9 is 16
Let's say them over and over again.

7+7 is 14
7+8 is 15
7+9 is 16
You won't hear the answers,
but say them again.

7+7 is...
7+8 is...
7+9 is...

(Chorus 2x)

Over and over again.
Over and over again.

©Twin Sisters Productions, Inc. TWIN 443 - Addition

While We Exercise

We're learning our facts three at a time.
We're learning our facts while we exercise.
Get out of your seats. Let's run in place.
It's time to learn the facts of eight.

(Repeat)

8+1 is 9
8+2 is 10
8+3 is 11
Make sure to breathe that oxygen!

We're learning our facts three at a time.
We're learning our facts while we exercise.
Now, jumping jacks are next in line.
Look alive! I want everyone to try.

8+4 is 12
8+5 is 13
8+6 is 14
You're looking like a lean machine.

We're learning our facts three at a time.
We're learning our facts while we exercise.
Now, touch your waist and then your toes.
Down and up; yes, that's how it goes.

8+7 is 15
8+8 is 16
8+9 is 17
What a splendid learning scene.

We're learning our facts three at a time.
We're learning our facts while we exercise.
No books or pencils are needed today.
Follow my lead. I'll show you the way.

Now one more time.
I'm not ready to stop.
Up and at 'em.
Let's take it from the top!

(Chorus)

8+1 is 9
8+2 is 10
8+3 is 11
Make sure to breathe that oxygen!

We're learning our facts
three at a time.
We're learning our facts
while we exercise.
Now, jumping jacks are next in line.
Look alive! I want everyone to try.

8+4 is 12
8+5 is 13
8+6 is 14
You're looking like a lean machine.

We're learning our facts
three at a time.
We're learning our facts
while we exercise.
Now, touch your waist
and then your toes.
Down and up; yes, that's how it goes.

8+7 is 15
8+8 is 16
8+9 is 17
What a splendid learning scene.

We've learned our facts
three at a time.
We've learned our facts
while we exercised.
Jumping jacks, and we ran in place,
touched our toes,
now we know the eights!
(Repeat)

©Twin Sisters Productions, Inc.

TWIN 443 - Addition

It's Time To Review

The facts of nine we've really gone through.
So I think, by now, it is time to review.
We know our facts from 0-8.
The nines are last. Isn't that great?

It's time to review.
It's time to review.
For we know the facts, isn't it true?
Addition is easy if we strategize.
Learning the rules helps us memorize.

9+1 is 10
9+2 is 11
9+3 is 12
9+4 is 13
9+5 is 14
9+6 is 15
9+7 is 16
9+8 is 17

One more fact, and I'll say it now.
It's 9+9, which is 18. Wow!

The facts of nine are easy to know.
Say them again—and we'll take it slow.
We know our facts from 0-8.
The nines are last. Isn't that great?

(Chorus)

9+1 is 10
9+2 is 11
9+3 is 12
9+4 is 13
9+5 is 14
9+6 is 15
9+7 is 16
9+8 is 17

One more fact, and I'll say it now.
It's 9+9, which is 18. Wow!

(Chorus)

I'm Talkin' About Doubles

I'm talkin' 'bout doubles.
Now, doubles mean two.
Doubles, doubles, doubles.
I'm tellin' the truth.

If you learn about doubles
when you're learnin' to add,
you'll ace all your tests
and make your teacher glad.

**Doubles, doubles, doubles.
Now, doubles mean two.
Doubles, doubles, doubles,
doubles help you.
They'll help you learn quickly.
There are ten double facts.
Doubles, doubles, doubles.
We're talkin' doubly good math!**

Let's take 1 and double it. 2
Let's take 2 and double it. 4
Let's take 3 and double it. 6
Let's take 4 and double it. 8
Let's take 5 and double it. 10
Now we'll say our facts all over again.

1+1 is 2
2+2 is 4
3+3 is 6
4+4 is 8
5+5 is 10

(Chorus)

Let's take 6 and double it. 12
Let's take 7 and double it. 14
Let's take 8 and double it. 16
Let's take 9 and double it. 18

Let's take 10 and double it. 20
You've got the idea.
You're learnin' plenty.

6+6 is 12
7+7 is 14
8+8 is 16
9+9 is 18
10+10 is 20

(Chorus)

I'm talkin' 'bout doubles.
Now, doubles mean two.
Doubles, doubles, doubles.
I'm tellin' the truth.

Let's mix up the doubles.
You can do the math.
Doubles, doubles, doubles.
We're learnin' the facts.

3+3 is 6
6+6 is 12
9+9 is 18
1+1 is 2
7+7 is 14
5+5 is 10
2+2 is 4
10+10 is 20
8+8 is 16
4+4 is 8

(Chorus 2x)

Doubles Plus One

I want to teach you a strategy called "doubles plus one." If you know your double facts, like 2+2 and 6+6, you will find this strategy helpful. If you have a problem where one addend is one more than the other, you can think of doubles and add one more. Let's look at 3+4. In the problem 3+4, 4 is one more than 3. So double 3 and add 1. 3+3 is 6 and 6+1 is 7! That's it. Look at 4+5. Double 4 and add one more. 4+4 is 8 and 8+1 is 9. Great!

**Doubles plus one.
Doubles plus one.
Double the smaller number
and then add one. How fun!**
(Repeat)

1+2 is 3
Just double 1, which is 2, and add one more. 3

2+3 is 5
Just double 2, which is 4, and add one more. 5

3+4 is 7
Just double 3, which is 6, and add one more. 7

4+5 is 9
Just double 4, which is 8, and add one more. 9

(Chorus)

5+6 is 11
Just double 5, which is 10, and add one more. 11

6+7 is 13
Just double 6, which is 12, and add one more. 13

7+8 is 15
Just double 7, which is 14, and add one more. 15

8+9 is 17
Just double 8, which is 16, and add one more. 17

(Chorus)

Number Line Addition
(Sums to 10)

Addition Facts:

3 + 4 = 7
addends sum

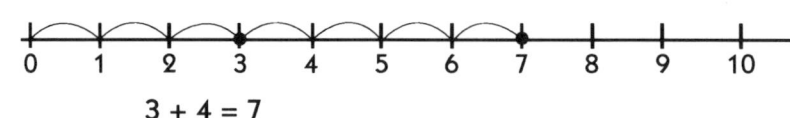

The numbers to be added are called addends.

The answer is called the sum.

Write an addition problem for what each number line is showing.
For example:

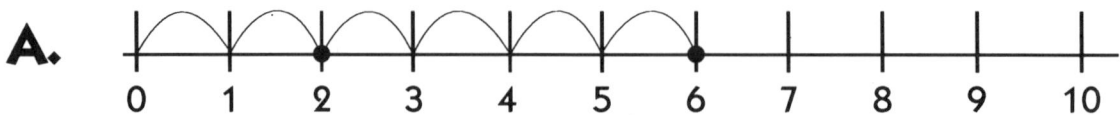

3 + 4 = 7

A.
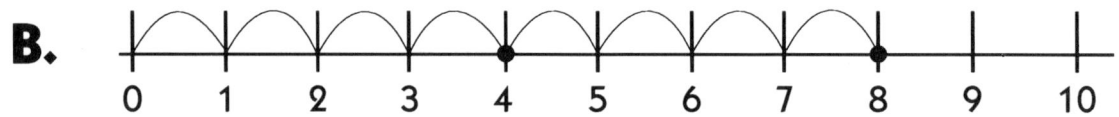

___ + ___ = ___

B.
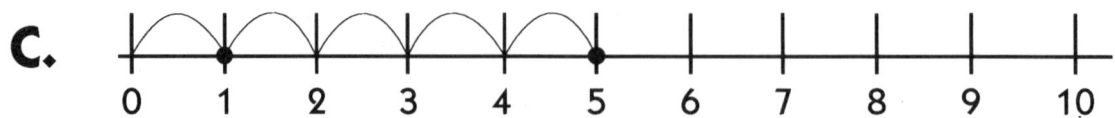

___ + ___ = ___

C.
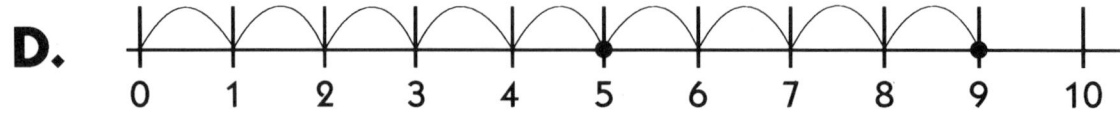

___ + ___ = ___

D.

___ + ___ = ___

Find The Secret Message
(Sums 0 to 12)

Find the secret message by placing the correct letter above the matching answer at the bottom of the page.

4 + 8 (P)	6 + 3 (R)	2 + 9 (S)	5 + 5 (A)
7 + 1 (T)	3 + 4 (W)	4 + 1 (E)	3 + 3 (H)
6 + 4 (A)	2 + 4 (H)	6 + 2 (T)	2 + 0 (I)
4 + 4 (T)	2 + 1 (F)	2 + 2 (C)	

__ __ __   __ __ __ __   __ __ __   __ __ __ __ __
9 10 12   7 2 8 6   8 6 5   3 10 4 8 11

©Twin Sisters Productions, Inc.   TWIN 443 - Addition

Greater Than/Less Than

Solve.
Write < (less than) or > (greater than) or = (equal to)

A. 6 + 3 ◯ 3 + 4   H. 7 + 3 ◯ 1 + 4

B. 7 + 2 ◯ 12 + 4   I. 5 + 12 ◯ 4 + 3

C. 4 + 3 ◯ 10 + 1   J. 10 + 3 ◯ 7 + 4

D. 6 + 5 ◯ 9 + 8   K. 6 + 2 ◯ 5 + 1

E. 2 + 13 ◯ 10 + 4   L. 1 + 3 ◯ 7 + 4

F. 5 + 11 ◯ 4 + 6   M. 5 + 5 ◯ 2 + 8

G. 1 + 1 ◯ 0 + 2   N. 6 + 3 ◯ 6 + 4

Adding Doubles

Add.

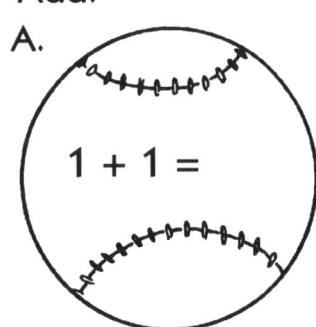

A. 1 + 1 =

B. 2 + 2 =

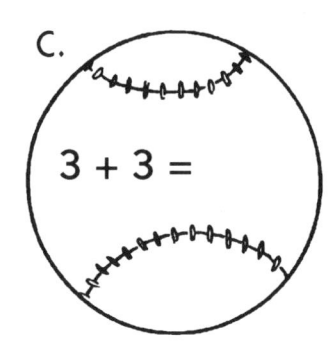

C. 3 + 3 =

D. 4 + 4 =

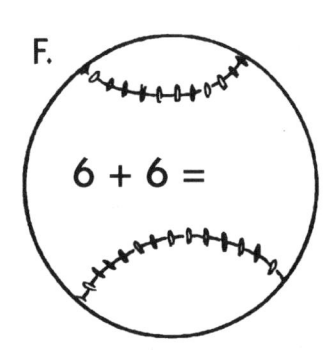

E. 5 + 5 =

F. 6 + 6 =

G. 7 + 7 =

H. 8 + 8 =

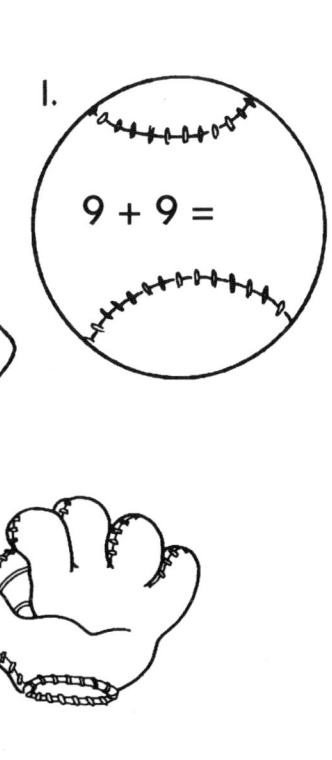

I. 9 + 9 =

J. 10 + 10 =

Doubles Plus One Practice

Strategy: If you have a problem where one of the addends is one more than the other, you can think of doubles and add one more. Just double the smaller number and then add 1.

Example: 4 + 5
Double 4, which is 8, and add one more, which makes 9
4 + 5 = 9

Practice using the "doubles plus one" strategy below.

3 + 4
Double 3, which is ____, and add one more, which makes ____
____ + ____ = ____

6 + 7
Double 6, which is ____, and add one more, which makes ____
____ + ____ = ____

2 + 3
Double 2, which is ____, and add one more, which makes ____
____ + ____ = ____

5 + 6
Double 5, which is ____, and add one more, which makes ____
____ + ____ = ____

8 + 9
Double 8, which is ____, and add one more, which makes ____
____ + ____ = ____

At The Baseball Game!

A. 3 new baseballs
   2 old baseballs

How many baseballs in all?
_____ + _____ = _____

B. 4 light bats
   6 heavy bats

How many bats in all?
_____ + _____ = _____

C. 5 girls
   7 boys

How many children in all?
_____ + _____ = _____

D. 8 red baseball hats
   6 blue baseball hats

How many hats in all?
_____ + _____ = _____

E. 4 bags of peanuts
   3 bags of popcorn

How many bags in all?
_____ + _____ = _____

F. 2 baseball games on Monday
   1 baseball game on Tuesday

How many games in all?
_____ + _____ = _____

G. 9 home runs by the home team
   3 home runs by the visiting team

How many home runs in all?
_____ + _____ = _____

H. 5 baseball mits
   4 baseball mits

How many baseball mits in all?
_____ + _____ = _____

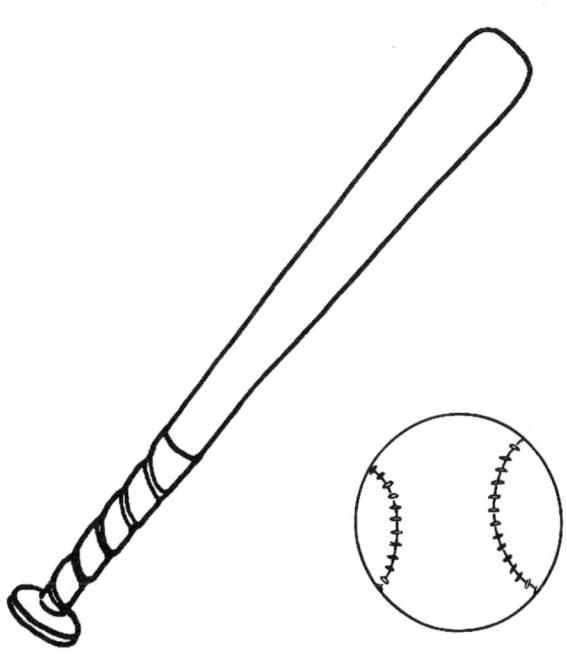

©Twin Sisters Productions, Inc.   TWIN 443 - Addition

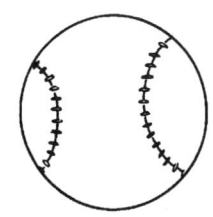

Time Test
Sums to 12

2 + 2	3 + 2	2 + 4	8 + 2	7 + 4	2 + 2

1 + 2	0 + 2	4 + 7	3 + 8	9 + 2	3 + 2

7 + 4	5 + 5	7 + 5	1 + 2	3 + 9	8 + 4

2 + 4	2 + 6	5 + 1	8 + 3	4 + 7	5 + 0

0 + 2	8 + 4	0 + 1	12 + 0	2 + 7	11 + 0

©Twin Sisters Productions, Inc.   TWIN 443 - Addition

Time Test
Sums to 18

2 + 0	8 + 4	0 + 5	5 + 5	4 + 5	12 + 2
2		5	10		

6 + 2	10 + 2	7 + 8	9 + 7	6 + 5	7 + 9

12 + 2	9 + 9	8 + 2	6 + 12	5 + 11	12 + 2

1 + 6	3 + 9	5 + 11	8 + 10	4 + 9	12 + 0

7 + 4	2 + 2	5 + 9	8 + 8	5 + 2	9 + 4

TWIN 443 - Addition

Answer Key

Page 16
A. 2 + 4 = 6
B. 4 + 4 = 8
C. 1 + 4 = 5
D. 5 + 4 = 9

Page 17
12, 9, 11, 10
8, 7, 5, 6
10, 6, 8, 2
8, 3, 4
RAP WITH THE FACTS

Page 18
A. >
B. <
C. <
D. <
E. >
F. >
G. =
H. >
I. >
J. >
K. >
L. <
M. =
N. <

Page 19
A. 2 B. 4 C. 6
D. 8 E. 10 F. 12
G. 14 H. 16 I. 18
J. 20

Page 20
A. 6, 7
   3+4=7
B. 12, 13
   6+7=13
C. 4, 5
   2+3=5
D. 10, 11
   5+6=11
E. 16, 17
   8+9=17

Page 21
A. 3+2=5
B. 4+6=10
C. 5+7=12
D. 8+6=14
E. 4+3=7
F. 2+1=3
G. 9+3=12
H. 5+4=9

Page 22
4, 5, 6, 10, 11, 4
3, 2, 11, 11, 11, 5
11, 10, 12, 3, 12, 12
6, 8, 6, 11, 11, 5
2, 12, 1, 12, 9, 11

Page 23
2, 12, 5, 10, 9, 14
8, 12, 15, 16, 11, 16
14, 18, 10, 18, 16, 14
7, 12, 16, 18, 13, 12
11, 4, 14, 16, 7, 13